Container Gardening

Patti Barrett

CONTENTS

Gardening in Containers

Gardening in containers gives the plant lover, no matter what size his garden may be, the extra gift of flexibility. Even if you have large flower and vegetable beds on your property, the importance of a few containers for instant color and drama wherever it's needed can't be underestimated.

If you live in a condominium, apartment, or small home where space is at a premium, container gardening takes on a new significance. Remember that you can, with patience and practice, grow almost any plant in almost anything that will hold soil. Not just a mix of petunias and geraniums for porch color, but anything you like: vegetables, fruit trees, lilies, shrubs, even small trees!

The choice — what you want to grow and what you want to grow it in — is yours. And one of the best parts of gardening in containers is that it's fun and easy to correct any mistakes. If your color combination didn't work out as you planned, you simply try again.

The only downside about container gardening is that it can become addictive. One beautiful container of plants usually leads to another and then another. Soon the pots will be taking over your terrace. Just remember to leave room for a chair so you can bask in the glory of your movable garden.

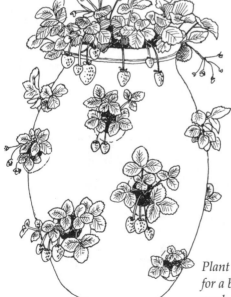

This book covers the basics of successful gardening in containers — how to plant and maintain in and around your house or apartment, on your balcony, terrace or patio, outdoor plants that might otherwise grow in a garden. It is aimed at both the seasoned gardener and the person who simply enjoys color and beauty around the home.

Plant strawberries in a terra cotta jar for a balcony or patio — a portable garden you can taste!

The sections that follow answer questions about what makes a good container and what makes a good plant for it; how to plant in containers; different mixes of flowers and vegetables; and how, once planted, to care for your container.

While we cannot cover everything in these few pages, we hope this will help you get started on what can become a pleasant pastime and rewarding occupation.

Containers

Let your imagination run wild when you think about what to use for a container. You are not limited to clay and plastic flower pots when you want to grow plants outdoors. Of course, these pots are basic, work well, and look fine in any garden scheme — but so do lots of other containers.

Traveling in Greece, I was amazed at the collections of potted plants by nearly every doorway. Every whitewashed house had a vivid collection of flowering plants and herbs growing in any kind of tin imaginable. Olive oil cans with the tops cut off were especially plentiful, and the plants looked lovely growing out of these colorful and practical containers. Grouped on a front step basking in the Mediterranean sun, the mixed array of cans one wouldn't normally associate with gardening seemed just right.

You can create a versatile, movable garden by placing flower pots in a child's wagon.

I tried the cans myself and, although they didn't look quite as well on my New England porch as they did in the hot reflected light of Greece, they did open my eyes to trying different types of containers. An old metal washtub I found at a flea market graces my front step with a colorful array of annuals each summer. That, along with an old ash bucket from a wood cook stove and a collection of other old buckets makes a display that looks just right with my Colonial home.

Once you begin looking, you will see that the choice of containers is limitless: large wooden boxes or tubs, half-barrels or boxes, large plastic pots, even garbage cans. A crate can be lined with a plastic bag or a wire basket can be lined with moss. Window boxes, hanging baskets, stone troughs, lead cisterns, and lovely antique urns can all be used as containers for your garden plants.

I know a small house in Michigan whose front yard has nothing but flowers growing out of the strangest assortment of items: old wheelbarrows, old red wagons and large wooden ones, watering cans, old wooden buckets and metal buckets and pots of every kind and description. For a house that has a small amount of land and soil that is mostly clay, it works.

The use of new materials such as concrete, artificial stone and plastics have added to our choice of containers. Large pots that look like pottery are made of plastic and have the advantage of being lighter and easier to move about.

Whatever pot you choose for your garden, there are a few rules to keep in mind. In any container, good drainage is a must. Excess water needs to come out of the container so that the plants' roots don't rot from the excess moisture. Plants will become weak if grown for any length of time in waterlogged soil. If you have a large attractive container that simply cannot be drilled, plant your plants in a smaller pot that fits inside.

Heavy containers are easier to manage if placed on a wheeled platform.

A container must be of an adequate size for the plant or plants that will be growing in it. If a pot is too small, the nutrients in the soil are used up too quickly or the plant could quickly become root-bound.

The material of the container is also important. The rate at which the potting mix will lose water is directly related to what the pot is made of. Soil in a terracotta pot dries out more quickly than does that in a plastic one, an important consideration when it comes to a plant's upkeep.

Daylilies will need frequent watering and a large pot to accommodate their roots.

Weight should also be considered. You don't want a container so light that it will blow over in a strong wind. And, while a pot that is too heavy to budge may serve as a focal point in the garden, you usually want something in-between. If you are in an exposed area that gets a bit of wind, be sure your container has a wide base to ensure stability.

Remember that once soil and compost are added to the container it gets much heavier! If you are gardening on a roof top or balcony you might need to consider a container made of a lightweight plastic that just looks like stone.

If you are converting something to be used as a container you may have to treat it so it lasts longer. You can extend the life of a wooden container by treating it with a preservative, but avoid those like creosote which are harmful to plants. You may want to treat cast iron pots with an anti-rusting material.

Pottery cannot be left out during a cold winter when the alternate freezing and thawing

Surround smaller pots in a larger one with peat moss, gravel, or perlite.

will cause the pots to crack. Move them inside or empty and store them under cover.

Pot color is even a consideration. In warm climates, light colored containers are better. Dark colored ones may absorb too much heat in the late-day sun.

Planting Mixes

The planting mixture is the most important part of container gardening. You will need a good mixture that is able to hold its nutrients and water even through hot, dry weather. Ordinary garden soil is usually too heavy for container gardening and it may contain insects and disease. It also tends to dry out quickly.

Many gardeners buy a prepared planting mix as they will not need more than a few cubic feet for their containers.

If you prefer, you can make your own planting mix. Keep three things in mind when creating your own: keep it economical, keep it lightweight, and — here's the tricky one — it should be moderately quick draining as well as able to retain moisture. No small order! But it can be done.

The planting mix needs to have a pH of 5.6 to 7.0 unless it's a specialized mix for acid-loving plants such as azaleas.

Whatever planting mix you decide on (see chart at right), the mixing process is the same. Dump the ingredients into a pile — on the ground or in a big wheelbarrow — and mix them roughly together. Dampen the mixture as you work with it. As you mix, add the ground limestone and fertilizer. Use fertilizer with nitrogen, potassium, limestone and the minor elements calcium, sulphur, iron, magnesium, zinc, copper, manganese and boron.

Extra planting mix can be stored in large plastic bags or plastic garbage cans.

Some gardeners prefer not using any garden soil in their mixes and choose instead the soilless mixes available commercially or make their own soilless mix. I prefer conditioning my own garden soil to make good container planting mix, but the soilless mixes are free of disease organisms and weed seeds.

Planting Mixes

Basic Mix:

1	part peat moss or compost (run through a screen)
1	part garden soil
1	part builders' sand

The organic material in this mix provides body, and the sand will improve drainage. Add extra peat moss for acid-loving plants; lime for plants that like neutral or slightly alkaline soil. Instead of sand, perlite or vermiculite can be used for drainage.

While mixing, add a slow-release fertilizer to the soil.

Soil-based Mix:

1	part sterilized loam
1	part medium grade peat moss, leaf mold, or tree bark
1	part coarse sand or perlite

Add balanced fertilizer.

Bulb Mix:

Use only for early forced bulbs — not enough nutrients for other plants

6	parts peat moss
2	parts crushed shell
1	part charcoal

Additions to Planting Mixes:

You can add many things to your planting mixes:

- Humus or leaf mold retains moisture well and gives the soil a nice texture
- Manure (use this in a dry, powdery form otherwise it will overpower the mix) is filled with nutrients
- Peat moss holds water and any added fertilizer well
- Limestone reduces acidity of potting mix
- Limestone chips reduce acidity and help with drainage
- Sand is good for drainage
- Perlite gives the mix an open texture which improves aeration and drainage (Use perlite instead of vermiculite if you get a lot of spring rain because it dries out faster.)
- Vermiculite absorbs and retains nutrients and moisture
- Sphagnum moss is excellent for water-retention

Mixes like Jiffy-Mix or Pro-Mix contain natural ingredients and are easy to use. They are also very lightweight which is a plus when you are lugging the pots around from one spot to another. A 2-cubic-foot bag of mix is enough 'soil' for 20 1-gallon containers or 35 pots 6 inches deep.

How to Plant

It is best to wet any medium well before using it. If you buy a pack-aged mix you can wet it right in the bag. Put water into the bag and knead it through until evenly moist. Let the mix rest overnight before you use it. Your own soil mix needs to be moistened well before using it, too.

Try to get your plants into their new container as soon as you can after purchase. Think about how you want them to look when they are grown. Know how tall and wide you can expect each to grow and arrange them accordingly.

Fill the containers with potting mix before you begin to plant. If they are heavy, be sure they are in their final position before you start.

Planting Tips

- Leave a 1½- to 2-inch headspace between the top edge of the container and the top of the soil. This allows you to water heavily without washing soil out of the top of the containers.
- Firm down the soil around the roots of the plants when you set them in place. This is simple to do with the heel of your hand or your fist.
- Set plants at least 2 inches from the edge of the container. This will help keep them from drying out.

When you bring your plants home, keep them moist. If your seedlings are in a plastic four- or six-pack, push them up from the bottom to remove for planting. If the plants are in a solid pack, use a sharp knife to cut through the planting mix to separate them. If your plant is in a single pot, hold the pot upside down, carefully supporting the plant, and tap on the bottom to remove the entire plant.

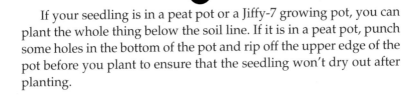

If your seedling is in a peat pot or a Jiffy-7 growing pot, you can plant the whole thing below the soil line. If it is in a peat pot, punch some holes in the bottom of the pot and rip off the upper edge of the pot before you plant to ensure that the seedling won't dry out after planting.

Fertilizing

Plants growing in containers need more attention than those in borders or the vegetable garden. Because of the limited volume of soil, the pot will dry out more quickly and need more added nutrients than the soil in the garden.

Even with a mix that has fertilizer added, you will have to fertilize again about three weeks after planting. And if you have had to water your container frequently, you'll need more fertilizer even sooner.

Some people prefer to feed with a weak solution of fertilizer every other time they water. Use about ⅕ the amount called for on the directions for a monthly application (if the directions call for 1 tablespoon of fertilizer to 1 gallon of water, you will use 1 tablespoon to 5 gallons of water).

Other gardeners fertilize less frequently, perhaps once a week, and still get good results. Still others swear they have to fertilize every time they water to ensure good flowering. These growers will often use a plant food such as Peters Professional Blossom Booster with a 10-30-30 rating and swear by it for lush flowers. You will have to experiment to see what you like. Hanging baskets sometimes benefit from more frequent feeding than other containers.

Most plants don't need large amounts of fertilizer but they do like to be fed on a regular basis. You may prefer using timed-release fertilizers instead of feeding with diluted solutions. As the plant receives water, these fertilizers are released in small amounts. The easiest method is to mix a timed-release fertilizer right into the soil you use. You can buy either 3-month or 12-month timed-release formulas.

The numbers after the name of the fertilizer indicate the percentages of available nitrogen, phosphorus, and potassium in each fertilizer. Many of the preparations include the minor elements as well. Some water soluble fertilizers are: Ra-pid-gro (13-26-13); Hyponex (7-16-19); Miracle-Gro (15-30-15) and Peters (10-30-20). Some slow-release fertilizers are Agriform (14-4-6); Mag-Amp (7-40-6); and Osmocote, available in several proportions.

Organic fertlizers such as fish emulsion are also effective.

Watering

Watering is the most important chore you will have to perform to keep the container plants healthy. The roots of your potted plants are not able to seek out water as they would if they were planted in the garden. Instead, they have to wait for you to provide it.

How much water your plants need depends on a number of factors: the nature of the soil; the temperature; the rainfall; the exposure of the plant to direct sun and wind; and the amount of growth of the plant.

Although we are usually concerned with the danger of a plant not getting enough water, with container gardening there is also the threat of a plant getting too much water — both can be detrimental to the plants' growth.

It is usually best to water in the early morning or the evening. Water the plant thoroughly — until the water comes through the drainage holes. Use your fingers to feel below the soil's surface. Water again when the soil is almost dry. Make sure you are watering the soil and not just the plant's leaves.

During the summer, check container plants morning and evening. Increased heat and sunlight dry out plants and soil more quickly. Even in the spring and fall pots can dry out quickly. And wind has a drying effect on plants as well.

You will soon learn when to water what. Some plants tell you immediately that they are thirsty. Impatiens, coleus and tomatoes will wilt dramatically when they need water, but usually recover just as quickly.

Learn to feel what your plants need. A plant may need water every day during a sunny week but only every other day when it's cloudier outside.

The type of container will also have a bearing on how often a plant needs water. Plants in porous clay pots need water more often than those in plastic or glazed ones. Some gardeners plant in a plastic pot and sink the plastic pot in a clay one to minimize watering needs. The space between the pots is insulated with peat moss, gravel, or perlite.

Another trick is to group small potted plants together in a larger box. This slows evaporation and decreases the frequency of watering. You can, again, put peat moss or another material between the pots.

Watering cans are most often used for watering plants in containers but many attachments available for the garden hose are invaluable for the container gardener. Rigid extensions that direct a flow of water above head height are useful for hanging plants; mist spray nozzles can give plants the humidity they need; and water breaker nozzles can deliver a high volume of water without disturbing the soil in the container.

However you water, make sure your plants are not sitting in water. Quickly remove excess water from the dish under the plant, if there is one. If you cannot lift the plant to do this, siphon water out with a baster or some other device. Root-killing mineral salts build up in standing water.

On Vacation

Many gardeners go away in the summer while their container plants are in full bloom and in full need of attention. If you can't find someone to water your plants, there are a few things you can do to keep them happy while you're away.

Move the plants to a shaded or protected spot, and water thoroughly right before you leave.

You can rig up your own reservoir to help water plants while you are gone. Wick watering will usually keep plants wet for about a week. Simply put one end of the wick in a pail of water and the other end in the soil of the pot. Specially made wicks are available in most garden centers or you can make your own out of a nylon clothesline, fraying the end that goes into the soil.

Pests and Problems

This book is too small to cover all the possible things that could bother your plants, but, by taking a few preventive steps, you can avoid many diseases and thwart potential pests.

Start with healthy plants, plant them in a clean mix in clean containers, grow them in the conditions they prefer (sun, shade, etc.), and water carefully.

When plants in containers are attacked by a bug or a disease you may have to be more ruthless than if you were handling the same problem in a garden. If the problem is found on only one plant it may be best to simply discard the entire plant, roots, and soil, before the affliction spreads.

With container plants it is easier to pick off larger bugs by hand than to deal with poisons. Caterpillars, snails, slugs, etc. are easy to spot and remove.

Smaller pests such as aphids and whitefly are harder to deal with. They can cause stunted growth and spread viral diseases. These can be controlled by a variety of sprays.

Mildew and black spot are apt to be found on some of your flowers, such as roses and nasturtiums, and can be controlled by spraying with a fungicide.

My pots are bothered most by water-seeking insects such as earwigs and slugs. They love being under the plant, especially making a home under the dish beneath the pot!

If you use slug bait you may want to put it on a leaf near the ground. Lay your trap in the early evening after wetting the area around and underneath the containers. In the morning you can catch your critters and dispose of them.

When watering, check over the leaves for any damage and under the pot for insect infestation. Treat immediately to avoid further problems.

Hanging Baskets and Window Boxes

Two of the favorite ways to display container plants are in hanging baskets and window boxes. Hanging baskets can brighten a dark exterior or turn a porch into an instant garden. Window boxes have, for centuries, brightened homes and apartments the world over with their abundance of bloom in a small space. Both of these plantings require some attention that is different than that given to other plantings.

Hanging Baskets

A hanging basket can be either one glorious plant grown to perfection or a grouping of plants that can resemble a living flower arrangement.

Once filled, a hanging basket can be very heavy. Make sure the connection is strong. Hang the basket directly from a beam or ironwork, or make sure the bracket you attach it to is securely fastened. Also be sure you can reach it easily for watering and fertilizing.

Placing the container so that it will look good is also important. One basket may work as a focal point, or you may want a line of baskets along the porch. Baskets may hang in a straight line or at various levels. Practice the placement with empty containers, and get the system ready before you plant. This will save a great deal of effort and time.

A wide range of containers can be used for hanging baskets — anything from plastic pots sold for the purpose to open wire baskets to a colander. An open framework allows you to place plants at

Fuchsia is a good choice for a hanging basket in a shady spot.

different levels in the basket. Then, when the plants have matured, the basket will be hidden from view and be glorious all around. Some baskets have one flat side so they can be attached to walls.

Different materials can be used to line an open basket for planting. Supplies of sphagum moss are dwindling in the wild, so I try to use other mosses that I collect around my home. You can also slit plastic with a sharp knife and insert the plants in the holes at different levels.

Planting a Wire Basket

1. First select and prepare the plants you are going to plant. Buy rooted cuttings, since these smaller specimens are easier to put through the basket's walls. Water well and allow the cuttings an hour to fill with moisture. Then slip each root ball from its pot and separate the plants by cutting with a knife.

2. Line a 12- to 14-inch wire basket with sphagnum moss halfway to the top edge. It is best to soak the moss first in a bucket of water.

3. Take a 24-inch circle of black plastic sheeting and cut a short slit in the center for draining. Lay the plastic over the moss in the basket. Add some potting mix and plant three or four vine-like or trailing plants to come out of the basket at this level.

4. Continue lining the basket with moss. At even spaces, work more plants through the frame, adding potting mix as you go.

5. Complete lining the basket with moss and finish planting from the top, filling with soil to just below the rim. Water thoroughly.

The care of this type of basket is similar to other hanging pots, except that it will need more frequent watering as moisture will also evaporate through the sides. Moss baskets can leak — when you water, you may want to move your plant or set a bucket underneath it to catch the drips.

There are many plants to choose from for hanging baskets. A few bushy plants will give a domed effect. Impatiens, geraniums, pansies, and fuchsias sprawl rather than get leggy.

Along with bushy plants, trailers are great for a real showpiece. Begonias tend to trail as do *Campanula isophyla*, *Lysimachia nummulania*, lobelias, nasturtiums, and verbenas.

Foliage plants such as ivies and *Helichrysum petiolatum*, and house plants such as *A. setaceus*, aspargus fern and the variegated foliage of Tradescantia pendula also work well. You can mix to your heart's delight and come up with some fascinating combinations.

Ferns do especially well in the shade and can be mixed with other plants in hanging pots or used alone. Some perennials, such as the ones mentioned earlier, can also be used. Lady's mantle can work as a good foil for other plants.

Vegetables can also work in hanging pots. Try the bush zucchini or a bush cucumber. Small-sized tomatoes can be grown in hanging baskets, too. Be sure they are well-fed.

Keeping any hanging container neat requires work. Constant pruning and dead-heading are needed. Pin shoots where you want them, or to the moss to encourage growth. Water before the foliage droops, and feed when needed.

At the end of the season, discard the plants and soil and save the moss and frame. Clean the moss of any soil or plants and store it in a plastic bag until you are ready to use it again.

Save your pots and baskets, too. Plan to start early the next spring growing your own hanging baskets.

A combination of bushy and trailing plants make a good hanging display.

Window Boxes

Perhaps the favorite container garden is the window box. Nothing makes one "ooh" and "aah" more than walking down a city street and seeing a colorful display of flowers cascading out of a window box. They brighten the town as well as the mood of everyone who happens to walk by.

A window box perched below a window can be enjoyed from inside as well as outside the home. And, for many, it may be the home's only garden.

Planting window boxes is easy. Just remember to keep them well-planted and full. They can even change with the seasons: spring bulbs can be followed by summer flowers, autumn mums, and winter greens. Or you can plant window boxes with herbs, small shrubs, or rock-garden plants.

Wood, plastic, and metal window boxes are available. Redwood, oak, elm, and cedar are good choices. Painting the inside of the boxes with a preservative will extend their life.

Choose a subdued color for your window box unless you plan to make a very dramatic statement.

Boxes made of wood fitted with metal or plastic liners are a good idea, especially if you plan to change your display. When one display has finished you can quickly change to the next with an already-planted liner.

A window box is usually 6- to 8-inches deep and wide. A porous soil mix should be used for planting, and adequate drainage holes are necessary.

Put heavy window boxes in place before planting. Line the bottom of the box, or liner, with coarse material such as pieces of broken pots or small stones. Partially fill the box with a soilless or other lightweight mix.

Remove plants from their containers and, as they are planted, work the soil mix around them, eventually topping off the mix just below the rim of the box. Don't water until the box is where you want it.

Many of the same plants that work well in hanging baskets will do well in window boxes. Standbys for shade are: begonia, impatiens, coleus, caladium, browallia, pansy, fuchsia, and ferns. For sun: petunias, geranium, lobelia, alyssum, ageratum, and nasturtiums. Spring showings are lovely with 'Tete-a-Tete' dwarf daffo-

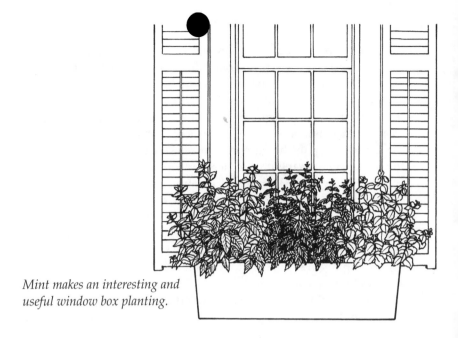

Mint makes an interesting and useful window box planting.

dils, Dutch crocus and hyacinths, or a mix of scillas and miniature irises.

If you want a long-term planting in a window box, try miniature evergreen shrubs. Some of the dwarf conifers are excellent and come in a wide range of colors and texture. Combine them with ivies or flowering plants for an unusual display.

Herbs do well in window boxes and prefer a sunny spot. And why not vegetables? Try some of the salad crops, such as lettuce in different shades mixed with radishes, and some of the newer varieties of vegetables available in miniature size.

Flowers for Containers

Flowers are the most common plant found in containers. Annuals, perennials, and bulbs can be found blooming in pots of all shapes and sizes, brightening up terraces and garden corners where other plantings won't work.

Annuals are flowers that sprout, mature, bloom, and die all within a single growing season. Perennials endure season after season. Both will work in containers. Bulbs are planted in the fall and wintered over for spring bloom. These take extra care but will also work in planters.

Vines can also be grown in containers. Some vines prefer to drape luxuriantly over the edges of their pots while others need the support of a trellis or line to grow around.

The combinations of different flowers are endless and are limited only by your imagination and budget. A container is a great place to experiment with different color combinations that you may be afraid to try in the garden. If it doesn't work, you can simply move it or replace it with another plant.

Many flowers perform well in containers if they are well watered and fed. Most people prefer annuals to perennials in containers because they offer a longer bloom period and only have to be maintained for one growth season. But perennials are often grown as annuals, especially in certain areas of the country. Geraniums, for example, grow year-round in southern California while in New England they are annuals.

Thoughtful use of color is a big part of the success of container gardening. It is easy to go overboard. Consider the colors you are using not just in one container but in containers you may group together.

Blue and yellow work well for summer and spring plantings — daffodils mixed with early pansies, forget-me-nots, or grape hyacinths. In summer the lobelias and campanulas can add blue shades to yellow pansies or pale yellow marigolds.

Single color plantings also work well. One big pot filled with a dense flowering of grape hyacinths, for example, can be most effective. Follow this with a single planting of impatiens to brighten a shady corner.

Color mixes are endless. A planting of ivy-leaved geraniums, lobelias, and gray-leaved helichrysum can be lovely in a summer garden.

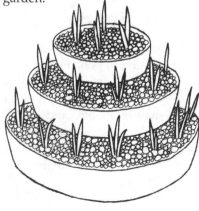

You can make an impressive display of bulbs by stacking containers on top of each other.

Foliage plants do well mixed with other garden flowers or simply left alone. A big pot of English ivy (*Hedera helix*) can be an elegant statement that can be moved indoors in the winter. Or mix the ivy with flowering plants such as fuchsia for an exciting scene stealer.

Any combination of flowers in "hot" colors such as reds and bright pinks can be lightened by a touch of white. Try white petunias with purple or blue flowers.

A good foliage plant can be a foil for flower color and can tone down a brightly colored plant. Ivy works well with most plants and has a wide range of leaf size and color, ranging from a golden yellow to a variegated leaf to white.

Foliage gives a certain depth as well as color. It helps give body, too, when flowers are between blossom times. Foliage can even be the main part of the planting. Some of the gray-leafed plants are wonderful in shade plantings, and large-leaved plants such as hosta can be the focal point of a planting or can be planted singly to shine in their own right.

The amount of light available has a great deal of bearing on the type of flowers that will do well in your containers. The ideal spot gets some shade during the day but also gets sun for at least half the day. This may be difficult to find!

Many containers are placed near buildings so there's usually quite a bit of shade to deal with. One way to increase the light in an area is to paint the walls behind the plants white. If this isn't possible, plant flowers that like shade.

Wind can be a problem for container plantings. If you have a particulary exposed spot, look for plants that are short and sturdy. Taller varieties can be damaged by wind. A few tulips on long stems will be shattered by a quick wind but the sturdier lower-stemmed hybrid tulips won't mind the breeze.

Bulbs

Bulbs can give early spring color and brighten any terrace or city container garden with their profuse bloom. Bulbs can also give summer and fall color, and when massed in pots are an impressive statement.

Plant lots of bulbs but stick to one variety per pot. Group the pots together for the look you want. Read the information that comes with the bulbs carefully.

Containers for bulbs need to be at least two inches deep and should have a good drainage hole.

1. Make sure your bulbs are properly labeled; keep the varieties separate and know the length of time it takes for each to bloom.

2. Check containers. Cover drainage holes with screen or curved pieces from a broken flower pot to prevent the planting mix from draining out of the pot.

3. Place a packaged planting mix in the pot so that the tops of the bulbs will be one inch below the rim when they are planted.

4. Place the bulbs close together in the pot. Tuck them in place so they are firmly settled in the soil.

5. Cover the bulbs with more mix.

6. Water the pots thoroughly. They are now ready to be stored in the cold, a necessary step for bulb growth.

7. Place the pots where they will get 12 to 14 weeks of temperatures between 40° and 50° F. Choose a spot that is dark and cold. Garages can work, or unheated basements or root cellars. If you live in an area where it doesn't get cold in the winter you may try storing your bulbs in the refrigerator.

8. Keep the bulbs moist during this period. Mist or water as needed but be careful that the soil doesn't get too wet, causing the bulbs to rot.

9. At the end of 12 to 14 weeks, when the sprouts are about three inches high and the roots are well developed, you can place the pots in a cool room — about 60°F. Or move the bulbs outside for normal growth.

I have planted tulips, daffodils, and crocus successfully in containers. Lilies are a summer flowering bulb that work very well in pots and are impressive in any garden setting.

Other Bulbs to Try

Allium. Many species come in a wide range of colors and sizes. Plant in the fall for spring to summer bloom. Some of the smaller ones are excellent for containers.

Begonia, tuberous. Plant in the winter for spring/summer bloom. These are luscious plants that like to grow in filtered shade. They come in all shades.

Crocus. Plant in the fall for early spring bloom. Many varieties grow to a height of four to five inches. The small bulbs just get covered with soil.

Dahlia. A summer delight, they have many flower colors and forms. The shorter varieties work best in containers. Plant in spring for summer bloom.

Hyacinth. Plant in fall for early spring bloom. Fragrant.

Lilium. Many flower forms and colors. Catalogs will tell you which work best in containers. Avoid the really tall varieties. Need good drainage and lots of moisture. Blooms in late spring throughout summer.

Narcissus. Plant in fall for spring bloom. Many shades and shapes and blooming times. The dwarf varieties make excellent potted plants.

Tulips. Plant in fall for spring bloom. Many colors and varieties to choose from. Most require at least five weeks of cold period. Look for varieties that work well in containers.

Annuals

Annuals are the mainstay of the container garden. If one plant comes to mind when you think of a potted outdoor plant it is probably the petunia or geranium. These can be found in almost any neighborhood, on any porch or windowsill, because they have characteristics that are good for container growing — they are colorful, tolerant of some dryness, and are long-lasting with simple care.

Petunias, geraniums, and marigolds like the sun. So do lantana and verbena, which will give extended bloom if kept cut back.

Popular choices for the shade are impatiens, wax begonias, fuchsia, and tuberous-rooted begonias. Fuchsia and tuberous begonias need shade all day long in July and August because the summer sun may burn their tender foliage. Be sure they are grown in a rich soil that can retain moisture. Too often store-bought hanging plants are grown in a peat-rich mix that won't hold the moisture. Sometimes you are better off re-potting the plant when you get it home.

Impatiens needs constant moisture as well as shade, though the newer varieties will tolerate some sun. Try mulching these potted plants to help reduce moisture loss.

Wax begonias seem to look healthier in shade but will also grow in the sun. Prune them back and remove spent flowers to keep them growing well.

Nasturtiums are another colorful choice for containers. A big pot of nasturtiums thrives all summer long on my sunny patio.

Flowering vines are good choices for containers as they can drape down or be trained up a trellis with other plants blooming below. Star-of-Bethlehem (*Campanula isophylla*) likes cool summers and its blue or white flowers look lovely; the black-eyed-Susan vine, (*Thunbergia alata*), is also pleasing with its lively orange flowers. Morning glories do well in containers and vinca vines look graceful when planted in window boxes or raised pots.

Gray-Leafed Plants to Add Accents

Dusty Miller *(Senecio cineraria)*. A favorite to mix. Leaves cut in lobes. Grows to 12 inches.

Curry Plant *(Helichrysum angustifolium)*. Becoming more popular — grows like lavender but has a curry scent. Looks good mixed with other plants.

Gray Santolina *(Chamaecyparissus)*. Finely cut leaves and lovely color make it a great addition. It can even be trained to grow like a small tree or it can spill over the edge of a container. Great for window boxes.

Perennials

Perennials are used less frequently in containers because of their shorter blooming period. But they can add a special effect, even though it may a short-lived one. A gorgeous delphinium planted in a big pot with annuals around it can make a dramatic statement.

A smaller perennial, lady's mantle, can look pretty all summer long and its graceful leaf shape and color will add to a mixed planting. The delicate pink flowers of coral bells also work well in containers as do shasta daisies or some of the garden geraniums that bloom almost all summer long. (Not to be confused with what we call geraniums — pelagoriums.)

Perennials need the same kind of care as annuals — lots of moisture, a good soil base, and fertilizer. If you want them to last for the next season, use a container that can withstand the winter weather — a large wooden box or metal container perhaps. Perennials need to be cut back in the winter and given some kind of protection. Often, however, perennials grown in containers are treated as annuals and discarded at the end of the growing season.

Flowers for Growing in Containers

Plant	Bloom Season	Colors	Light	Comments
Ageratum	Su – F	Blues and white	Sun, part Sh	Plant a few in a window box or mix with marigolds in planter.
Alyssum	Sp – F	White mainly, also purples	Sun, part Sh	Fast growing, low growing-profuse bloomer. Useful in hanging mixtures; good as ground cover in planting of small standard.
Begonia, fibrous	Su – F	Many – pinks, roses, whites	Sun to full Sh	Works well in all kinds of planters. Mixes well with fuchsias, lobelias, coleus. Look for Avalanche series for hanging baskets
Begonia, tuberous	Su – F	Wide range	Filtered shade	Likes it cool with high humidity. Bulb — plant in winter.
Browalia	Su – F	Whites, lavenders	Sh to light sun	Blooms profusely: hanging baskets, pots, window boxes.
Campanula	Su	White, blues, lavenders		Long bloom, C. isophylla especially good for hanging baskets.
Coleus	Su – F	Wide variety of foliage color	Light Sh	Grown for leaf color. Pots, hanging baskets, window boxes.
Dahlia	Su – F	Many	Sun	Many colors and different blossom shapes and sizes. Start from tubers. Excellent for different containers — not especially for hanging baskets unless small and mixed
Fuchsia	Su	Pinks, crimson, purples often mixed with white	Sun to part Sh	Different varieties good for all types of pots. Trailers excellent in hanging baskets.
Geranium	Can bloom all year (bring indoors in cool climates)	Pinks, reds, white, salmons, combinations	Sun; can take some shade	All containers. The standby. Mixes well with many plants

Plant	Bloom	Color	Light	Notes
Impatiens	Su – F	White, crimson, many pinks, orange, bicolors	Shade – New Guinea varieties will take sun	One of stars of containers — especially for all-season bloom in shade; hanging baskets and all kinds of pots. Mix with fuchsia
Lobelia	Su – early F	Blues, white	Sh to part sun	Trailing and upright forms. Good in all types of containers.
Marigold	Su – F	Yellows, orange, solids and bicolors	Sun	Profuse bloomer, sizes for all types of containers; easy care.
Nasturtium	Su – F	Yellow, orange, reds, creams, bicolors	Sun	Likes dry soil, not too rich. Different varieties — some great trailers; good for all pots.
Nicotiana	Su – F	Reds, white, green shades	Sun to part Sh	Grows well in pots, window boxes. Likes some shade in hot areas. Some varieties fragrant.
Pansy	Sp – F	Wide range and combinations	Sun to part Sh	Many uses in pots of all kinds — effective for early spring display. Also known as violas — the smaller flowered variety.
Petunia	Su – F	Wide range, singles, doubles, bicolors	Sun	Another mainstay of container plantings. All containers. Mixes well with other plants — especially pansies and marigolds.
Portulaca	Su	Mixed colors	Sun	Trailing plant good for hot, dry locations. Likes shallow pots and hanging baskets — and window boxes
Salvia	Su – F	Red, blue, pink and white	Sun to part Sh	Excellent container plant; good in large pots or mixed plantings or alone. Try the scarlet to attract hummingbirds
Thunbergia	Su – F	Orange, yellow	Sun	Trailer, excellent for hanging baskets or when given support to grow up — or window boxes.
Verbena	Su – F	Reds, pinks, blues, whites	Sun	Bush type is best. Profuse bloomer. All pots.
Vinca	Sp	Blue or white	Sun to Sh	Evergreen foliage good as filler in planters, and hanging baskets or beneath small tree-like specimens.
Zinnia	Su – F	Wide range	Sun	Shorter varieties work well in pots in full sun. Not hanging.

Vegetables in Containers

If you don't have the space for a vegetable garden, you can still grow vegetables in containers. They'll be portable, they can be turned to face the sun, and they can even be brought inside if a sudden storm threatens. And, vegetables are attractive while growing.

Container-grown vegetables are subject to the same problems as all container-grown plants — they dry out quickly and need frequent feeding. But, given care, vegetables in pots are worth the extra effort.

While you can try almost anything in containers, you may want to stay away from large plants like sweet corn, as the yield isn't great and the space required is considerable. It is better to choose vegetables with relatively small root systems — peppers, tomatoes, lettuce, onions, carrots, and eggplants.

Vegetable containers tend to be larger than those used for ornamentals — from three to 30 gallons. Anything smaller and the plant will dry out too quickly and there won't be enough room for root development.

Think about your needs before choosing or building your containers. You may need a series of boxes if you are going to grow a variety of crops. Boxes that are eight inches deep and two by three feet are good for vegetables such as beets, carrots, zucchini, and onions.

For vegetables that will grow up a trellis, try an 8-inch- deep box that is narrow — one foot by four feet.

And, for those crops you grow singly, such as tomatoes, peppers, and eggplant, use pots that hold four to five gallons.

Once you have your containers, fill them with your soil mix (see page 7). Remember that pot-grown vegetables need super soil. Be sure to add a slow-release fertilizer to the mix.

It is easy to transplant young seedlings to containers. Leave a 1- to 2-inch headspace so you can water heavily without washing soil out of the top of the container. Firm the soil around the roots of the young plants, and set them back at least two inches from the edge of the container to keep the roots from drying out.

Choosing the Vegetables

Certain kinds of vegetables are made for container growth. Small, fast-growing greens such as lettuce, kale, Swiss chard, and New Zealand spinach are good choices. Fruiting vegetables that produce over a long period are excellent choices — tomatoes, peppers, eggplant, and summer squash. Compact-vined muskmelons also work well in containers.

Combinations can work, too. Try fast-growing vegetables around the slower ones. For example, some leaf lettuce grown around an eggplant or tomato.

Read your seed catalogs carefully for information on which varieties work well in containers. Then, either look for these varieties in the market, or, if you have the space and time, start your own.

You can grow an entire vegetable garden in containers! Clockwise from top: beans on a teepee; tomatoes; lettuce, carrots, and spinach; herbs (parsley and basil); peppers; and cucumber.

VEGETABLES FOR CONTAINERS

Beets

Detroit Dark Red, Golden Beet. Likes cool weather; plant in spring or fall. Will tolerate some shade. Container should be at least 8 inches deep.

Broccoli

Green Goliath, Bonanza hybrid. Plant in spring. Likes full sun. Grow in container at least 8 inches deep.

Cabbage

Ruby Ball, Stonehead Hybrid. Needs cool weather to mature. Likes full sun. Any kind of container 12 inches deep.

Carrots

Short-rooted varieties such as Nantes Half-long, Royal Chantenay, Little Finger. Plant in spring, summer, or fall. Thin early to 3 inches apart. Loose soil, at least 10 inches deep.

Cucumbers

Bush type is good, such as Spacemaster; or with longer vines, train up on a trellis. Plant in a narrow, 8-inch deep box. Likes full sun. Grows well in summer.

Eggplant

Dusky Hybrid, an early variety. Needs full sun and warmth to grow well. Plant one to a 5-gallon container.

Kale

Different varieties. Will tolerate some shade. Plant in 8-inch deep container. Grows best in cooler weather. Harvest whole plants or the outside leaves.

Lettuce

Choose varieties that are slow to bolt in heat: Slobolt, Oakleaf, summer Bibb. Plant in early spring or fall. Will stand partial shade. Give head lettuce space, at least 10 inches apart in an 8-inch deep box. Leaf lettuce can be closer together. Harvest as needed.

Melons

Cantaloupes: Muskateer, Bush Star. Watermelon: Burpee's Sugar Bush, Yellow Baby Hybrid. Full sun. One plant per 5-gallon container. Needs summer heat.

Onions

Use as green spring onions or let mature. Plant in early spring. Container needs to be at least 6 inches deep. Green onions will take some shade; full sun needed for mature onions.

Peppers

Many varieties of sweet bell and hot peppers. All look good and are easy to grow in containers. Full sun. Plant in late spring, early summer. One plant to a 3-gallon container.

Radishes

Cherry Belle, Icicle, and Scarlet Globe are old favorites that do well in pots. Plant in spring or fall. Likes full sun. Any size container. Mixes well with other plants. Harvest early.

Spinach

America and Melody Hybrid are good for pots. Plant in spring or early fall. Needs full sun; can stand some shade. Any size container. Mixes with other greens or onions.

Swiss Chard

Rhubarb chard is very pretty with its red stems. Plant in spring, summer, or fall. Will stand some shade. Use any container that is at least 6 inches deep. Harvest again and again. Cut outer leaves and more will grow. Good replacement for early spinach.

Tomatoes

Burpee's Pixie Hybrid; Patio Hybrid; Small Fry; Super Bush and Tiny Tim. Needs full sun. One per 5-gallon container.

Zucchini, or summer squash

Compact varieties like Black Magic and Gold Rush. Plant in full sun. One plant per 5-gallon pot. Harvest when small. One plant will probably be all you will need.

Herbs in Containers

Herbs are so rewarding to grow — they respond to what little care you offer with glorious scents and flowers, and they can be used in many ways in the home. Even if you don't have space for an herb garden, you are sure to have room for a few pots of herbs, if not an entire herb garden in a planter.

Herbs do well in containers. They don't need much growing space and most, since they hail from warm climes, like to be in warm growing conditions.

Most herbs will grow well in individual containers. Try the sprawling herbs, such as spearmint or oregano, in a hanging basket. An effective moss-lined basket can be made with rooted cuttings of spearmint for a charming, scented delight.

Tarragon, sweet bay, rosemary, and winter savory like to grow in 12-inch pots with good drainage.

One box, one foot by four feet by eight inches deep, can be a self-contained herb garden with chives, thyme, parsley, basil, marjoram, and summer savory.

Window boxes that get sun are good for herbs. Try this mix: thyme, sage, coriander, and a prostrate rosemary. Judicious pruning for kitchen use should keep the box neat and tidy. An effective window box can be made of a mixture of thymes. Try the different shaded, leafed, and scented thymes in a sandy soil mix. With careful pruning and a little feeding this can be a perennial window box that will last for a number of years.

You can get a jump on spring if you grow herbs in a sunny window box. Plant frost-resistant varieties such as sage and winter savory and parsley.

Mints tend to be aggressive and are best grown in containers to restrict their ambitious roots. If you want them in a window box or other container, plant the mint first in its own pot so it doesn't take over.

Strawberry jars make effective planters for herbs. The pockets are good homes for some of the trailing herbs — try thyme, rosemary, or Alpine strawberries in the side with basil and sage planted on top. Or fill the whole jar with scented geraniums. When planting a strawberry jar, I like to insert a cone in the middle that I fill with perlite to keep the jar light. Soil goes around the sides and fills in the top opening where the plants will grow.

Be sure all herbs you plant in containers have excellent drainage. Water all herbs from the top. Many herbs like to have their leaves sprayed, and this helps to keep them clean.

HERBS FOR CONTAINERS

Small-leaved Basil
Grows smaller than the common sweet basil and does not become coarse as it ages. It is a tender annual. Pinch out the tops for general use. Try the opal basil for an unusual color.

Salad Burnet
A tidy plant with attractive leaves and small purplish red flowers. It has a shallow root system and likes very dry soil. Give it a sandy soil mix and add some lime to the pot.

Chives

Looks like grass in a planting, but purple flowers add to any box of herbs. Some, like garlic chives, have white flowers.

Dill

Dill has feathery green foliage on a single stalk that can get too tall for many plantings. But planted in a group of herbs and cut when needed, it will grow well.

Lavender

A favorite in any garden with its delightful smell and lovely purple flowers. Look for compact growing forms.

Marjoram

An attractive plant with small rounded leaves. Needs sunlight and air space for good growth. Cut leaves to prevent blossoming.

Parsley

Good herb for containers. Curly-leafed gives interesting texture to any mixture. Clip and use to maintain plant.

Lemon Verbena

Likes to be in pot; will bloom with white flowers. Sweet leaves good for tea.

Rosemary

Tender; take inside in winter. Prostrate form will fall nicely over edges of pots; likes a cool, sunny spot and occasional misting. Don't let dry out.

Sage

Sun and lime-loving, likes a bit of fertilizer and good drainage. Can grow quite large and draping with good care. Needs room. Different varieties, some with interesting variegated foliage.

Sweet Bay

Likes to summer outdoors, take inside in winter. Can grow quite large. Grow alone.

Tarragon

Mature tarragon needs room – at least an 8- or 10-inch pot if grown alone. Needs sun to do best but will take some shade. It likes dryish, well-drained soil – but don't let it dry out completely. Cut green leaves from the top or side growth.

Thyme

Many varieties of this plant, both creeping and upright, are excellent for container growth. Most flavorful are the lemon thymes and the French and English varieties. Some have woolly leaves, others have yellow foliage, and many will hang decoratively over the edge of a pot. All like full sun, light, limy soil, and good drainage.

Herbs for Fragrance

Geraniums *(Pelargonium).* Scented geraniums give wonderful fragrance just by brushing against their foliage. There are more than 250 species, so the choice is yours. Don't over-water geraniums — and never let them stand in water. They like frequent trimming to keep in line; pinch out the growing tops of young plants for a better shaped plant. Some to try: Rose, lemon rose, apple, lemon, nutmeg, peppermint — all good and fun to grow.

Lavender. One of my favorite plants. Likes well-drained or gravelly soil and sun. Try the different varieties. Clip to keep in shape.

Lemon Balm. Will grow to two feet. Leaves are crinkled and attractive. Likes to spread, so plant alone or in a pot sunk in a mix.

Grow an Herb as a Standard*

A standard is a shrub or tree that has been trained to a single stem with a bushy head. Bay, rosemary, geranium, sweet myrtle, santolina, lavender, and lemon verbena all can be grown as standards.

Start with a young plant or a well-established cutting. Choose a main upright stem and remove all other stems and leaves, except the growing tip.

As the plant grows, pinch back all new lower leaves, shoots and lateral branches. Tie the stem to a vertical support.

When the main stem reaches the desired height, pinch off the growing tip to stop the plant's upward growth. Allow leaves to develop to round out the top, but keep the lower stem clean of growth.

*From The Able Gardener: Overcoming Barriers of Age & Physical Limitations, by Kathleen Yeomans, R.N.